Terrib

MW00595832

Stopping Toddler Tantrums & Toddler Behavior Problems Quickly

Bowe Packer

TABLE OF CONTENTS

PUBLISHERS NOTES

Disclaimer

This publication is intended to provide helpful and informative material. Please understand, it is not intended to cover every single aspect about the terrible twos and toddler behavior problems. You will without a doubt run into certain things that I did not. This is the natural process of life.

However, with that said, I did my very best to cover all the aspect of this particular endeavor and I hope you will see that in the chapters of this book.

I, the author and publisher specifically disclaim all responsibility for any liability, loss or risk, personal or otherwise, which is incurred as a consequence, directly or indirectly, from the use or application of any contents of this book.

Any and all product names referenced within this book are the trademarks of their respective owners. None of these owners have sponsored, authorized, endorsed, or approved this book.

Always read all information provided by the manufacturers' product labels before using their products. The author and publisher are not responsible for claims made by manufacturers.

Paperback Edition 2013

Manufactured in the United States of America

DEDICATION

I dedicate this book to all those people out there who do not settle for mediocrity, those that hold themselves accountable for their life.

I know at times it may be difficult and you want to throw your hands up in the air and take no responsibility for what your life is.

I want you to know, I appreciate you and all your hard internal hard work. I know it isn't easy, however, the payoff is grand.

Thank you for being you and being vigilant to how you show up in the world.

Sent from LOVE,

Sunshine In My Soul

INTRODUCTION

Children are our pride and joy. They are the loves of our lives and we would do anything we possibly could to keep them happy and healthy. The problem arises when our children are not the perfect little angels that we would always like them to be and, instead, seem to go off the deep end into what most people refer to as 'the terrible twos.'

A period of time that is, not necessarily confined to the time period where your child is two years old, the terrible twos are a time of great difficulty for most parents. This is when your child starts to really have a mind of their own and when they start to think that they should have their way more often than you believe is necessary.

Throughout this book we will discuss the many different things that every parent should know about their child when they start entering the 'terrible twos.' All the information you will need to help your children (and yourself) get through this challenging stage is contained in two parts dealing with techniques for handling your child's behavior and how to understand and help them with the mental and emotional changes they are facing.

Each section of this book is arranged so that they can be read all together (thus you can read this book just like a book) or piece by piece. That means if you only need information about one aspect of the terrible twos say potty training for example, you can flip right to the potty training section and read from there. You can also refer back to this book quickly and easily for helpful reminders as your child passes through each of these milestones and events.

So let's jump in with both feet and both eyes open. The terrible twos are upon you or they're coming up fast and you definitely don't want to waste any time.

PART 1: CONGRATULATIONS, YOUR BABY IS A TODDLER

All right so you've made it through the first couple years with your new baby. You survived pregnancy, childbirth and that first year where you didn't know when you should switch to formula or what swaddling even meant let alone how to do it. You've survived, your partner has survived and your baby is thriving. So you've made it through the hard part right? Actually you couldn't be more wrong.

As anyone who has been a parent to a toddler will tell you there is much more to raising that toddler than there was to raising your infant. After all that infant wasn't capable of telling you no, throwing all-out temper tantrums or running off and getting into absolutely everything in sight (and half the things that aren't). You've probably heard all the whispers about those 'terrible twos' and thought 'my sweet child is never going to turn out like that. She's an angel.' Well just you wait.

So what are you going to do when your child starts getting into those terrible twos? Are you going to throw in the towel and say 'well there's nothing I can do about it?' No you're not. You're going to meet those dreaded years head on and do everything you need to make sure that your child is healthy and happy (and that you stay sane).

The first thing that you need to know is that it's completely normal. You're probably thinking, 'what's completely normal?' The answer is all of it. The way your child is acting is completely normal and the way you and your partner are going insane is completely normal. The fact that you don't know what to do and are looking for more help and advice is completely normal. So don't worry about those problems, you're doing the right thing, and before you know it you'll be helping your child the right way.

The next step to consider is discipline. No not punishment (or at least not necessarily). Discipline is ensuring that your child is doing what they are supposed to be doing. When you tell your child 'no' you are giving discipline. You're not punishing them, you're simply informing them that their actions are not what you want them to do. They learn without having to sit in time-out. This is what you should be striving for throughout your child's life. You want to teach them through positive discipline rather than through negative punishments.

Don't feel like you're in this alone. All parents go through that stage where they feel like they must have done everything wrong for their child to be acting this way. Read this next line very carefully. **You haven't done anything wrong.** There. Now you can breathe a sigh of relief and continue reading through this book to find out what you need to do from here on in to keep your child happy and yourself in control.

Chapter 1 - How Children Grow

What we want to look at first is how your child got to the stage that they are in now. This will help you to better understand the way that your child is growing and the way that they will continue to grow throughout their lives. This is also the way that you, me and every other human being on the planet will grow because it's evolutionary. Each of these stages will occur throughout the life of every person you come into contact with (so we really are essentially the same).

Each stage that we discuss here will talk about the age that the individual reaches it and what happens or needs to happen while they are there. If these things don't happen it can cause developmental difficulties and setbacks. It can also cause behavioral problems for the child which result in difficulties for the parent as well. This is why it's important to understand each level and what you should be doing to help your child at each one.

Note however, that the way your child develops is not entirely your fault. Though there is debate amongst researchers and scientists the effects of the environment that your child grows up in (outside of the home as well) has an influence on them and their upbringing.

STAGE ONE: INFANCY
Key Task: **Bonding**

When your child is only an infant you want to focus on the way that you bond with them. This will allow the two of you to be more comfortable together and will help your child to trust that you are there for them and that you will always provide for them. This is where your child will begin to understand that the world is a good place and that they can trust people.

By bonding with you through the affection and attention that you provide, your child will be gaining these skills which will help them to build relationships throughout their lives. This occurs from the time that your baby is born until they are approximately two years old.

Another thing to focus on however, is the way that you teach your child to interact with others. They will naturally bond with you as a result of the close association that you have. After all, you're the one who will be putting them to bed and feeding them and changing their diapers. It's nearly impossible for them not to form a relationship. But the way they feel about others will result from this initial relationship and the way that you teach them.

You want to provide that method of thinking that your children believe people are inherently good and that they can look to others to take care of their basic needs. This is a time where your child will either learn to trust the people in their lives or they will learn to mistrust them. If they learn mistrust it will be difficult for your child to form relationships with anyone in the future and they will constantly believe that they cannot depend on anyone.

STAGE TWO: TODDLER YEARS
Key Task: **Independence**

This is the stage where you are currently with your child. This is where your precious little angel turns into the screaming, fighting brat. Of course there are many reasons that these things happen. The very first thing that will occur at this stage is that your child will begin to feel more independent and will want to do things for themselves. This is instrumental in their growth and development and should definitely be encouraged, however it's important that you try to curb some of the rebellion that will likely occur.

Your child will, at this point in their life, learn that they can do things for themselves. If you stifle this ability you can actually cause them to stop doing anything for themselves and believe that they are unable. They will start feeling inadequate like they are incapable or unworthy of doing things for themselves. At this stage you want to allow your children more freedom to do or learn the things they are able to do and help them with the things they can't.

The terrible twos often occur because your child is trying out that independence. They have finally learned the word no and what it means and (after all that time having it used on them) want to try it out on you as well. They may refuse to eat foods they like or refuse to wear certain clothes or play with certain toys. They may insist on doing things themselves which could result in messes or temper tantrums when they don't get their way.

The first real milestone here is that your child begins walking. Right around the age of two this will happen though you shouldn't worry if your child starts walking as early as one year or as old as 2 ½. Children learn and grow at different rates and it's nothing to be concerned about. That first step is the signal that your child is reaching the terrible twos because once they start walking they can get where they want to go by themselves.

Your child wants to learn and explore their world and that's actually a good thing (no matter how many times you have to rewash the pots and pans or scrub crayon off the kitchen floor). Your child will begin to refine their gross motor skills and develop fine motor skills while they explore. Gross motor skills are things like walking or climbing (that's why you need gates in front of your stairs) while fine motor skills are holding objects or drawing.

Finally, you may notice that your child is beginning to speak more than they did before. Likely before the age of two and their entrance into toddlerhood your child was saying very few words and they were likely not stringing them together into sentences very often. Once your child gets to this stage they will start being able to have conversations (they will likely be short and may be quite random in nature) and they will be able to form rational thought processes (though not very complex ones.

While you've probably been trying to associate words with objects for your child for quite some time, now is the time that they will begin to actually understand those associations and realize that objects have their own names. They will also learn how to speak more quickly and likely pick up many new words every day. Don't use 'baby-talk' with your child especially at this stage. If you do then your child will learn how to talk that way and won't learn the proper words or pronunciations for objects in their world.

Another important thing to remember is to encourage your child to talk. They may start telling you about their lunch and then suddenly switch topics to talk about grandma and the last time they went to her house. The reason this happens is that your child is simply thinking and remembering the things that have happened to them. They want to talk and they want to share things with you. Encourage this and keep helping them learn new words as they go.

As your child talks they will be exercising their mind which will, in later life, allow them to do even more things like read, write, study and even play games. These things are the building blocks to all the learning they will do in the future and that means it's important that they learn and remember the skills necessary. Without being able to remember these things your child will not be able to associate objects with words or events the second or third time they come around.

At this stage your child will be developing their personality. This is when they start to think of themselves as an individual but at this point they can't understand that everyone else is not just like them. Therefore if they like the color blue then everyone must like the color blue. They can't understand also that when they pushed Billy on the playground, Billy was hurt. They don't know how to associate their own feelings with what Billy must be feeling.

Now we need to discuss punishment and discipline for your child. These things are both related to shame. Your child will feel shame when they are told that something they have done is incorrect or bad. When you scold your child for tearing a book they will feel shamed for the behavior and they will realize that what they did resulted in the negative action. This can hurt your child's self-satisfaction which occurs from their doing things on their own.

What you should remember however is that this is a temporary thing and that your child needs to learn the rules and the ways to do things that will help them through life. By teaching them the first time they are able to make changes to their behavior and adjust their self-satisfaction to fit the positive behaviors they are supposed to engage in.

CHAPTER 2- DEVELOPMENTAL MILESTONES

So what are developmental milestones? These are points in your child's life where they learn new things. Of course these aren't just any new things. At a developmental milestone your child is learning something that will prove instrumental in their future life. This could be walking, crawling, reading or speaking their first word. Of course these are some of the biggest milestones that we, as parents, can think of, however there are multiple different events that will occur.

Here we'll focus on the milestones that occur right around the time of the terrible twos so you can see what all is really happening for your child during this time. By understanding all the changes that are happening in such a small span of time it may be easier for you to realize just why your child seems to change overnight.

PHYSICAL MILESTONES

- Climbing onto/sitting on a chair
- Walking alone
- Throwing a ball
- Climbing stairs
- Feeding themselves
- Using utensils
- Drawing or coloring
- Standing on one foot

MENTAL MILESTONES

- Does things intentionally for a reason
- Remembers the past/thinks of the future
- Imagination develops (i.e. something can be used as something else)
- Imitation of others (i.e. playing house, mimicking parents)
- Realizes that everything exists whether it's in front of them or not

EMOTIONAL MILESTONES

- Nervous when left somewhere new
- Affectionate to friends and loved ones
- Effectively and accurately demonstrates emotion
- Ashamed of inappropriate actions
- Proud of appropriate actions
- Rapid mood changes
- Understands/anticipates danger
- Basic understanding of other people's feelings

AWARENESS MILESTONES

- Understands and responds to own name
- Wants to form friendships and relationships
- More assertive
- Understands environment
- Controls actions and behaviors

COMMUNICATION MILESTONES

- Use of complex words
- Uses combinations of words to form sentences
- Communicates wants and needs

PART 2: MAKING THE TERRIBLE TWOS BETTER THAN EVER

So now you know what is happening to your child and what they are going through as they grow from infants into toddlers. There are a lot of changes happening and there are a lot of things that they need to learn. You also know what happens if they don't learn those things. So now you're probably getting scared right? You're thinking about all those horror stories of children who turned two and went out of control. Well the great news is that with this next section we're going to teach you all about how to help your child skip right over those terrible twos.

So what's the first step to solving the terrible twos dilemma? Discipline. Now once again this doesn't mean punishment. What this means is teaching your children the difference between right and wrong without using aggression or letting them get away with it. The key is staying calm even when your child is not.

Key One: Focus on What Your Child Should do Not What they Shouldn't.
This means that you want to look at the way your child is acting and emphasize the good things they do as well as showing them how to do something the right way. For example if your child rips a page in a book you don't simply want to scold them. You want to show them how they should treat a book. Show them how to hold the book and 'read' rather than ripping pages.

Key Two: Limit Punishments Severely.

Don't punish your child for every tiny thing they do wrong. Remember discipline is not the same as punishment. A punishment will be less effective when carried out more and more often because your child will no longer see it as a punishment. Instead, limit punishments to only when they are absolutely needed to correct behavior that must immediately be stopped.

CHAPTER 3- RAISING YOUR CHILD THE BEST WAY POSSIBLE

Now there are more things involved in a healthy and happy child than just getting their way and eating good food. In fact, there are all different types of things you're going to need to look at and think about to make sure your child becomes a well-rounded adult. So what things can you do for your child? You want to give them all the benefits they could possibly have and help them as much as possible. Well there are a number of things that you can do for just that:

1. **Maintain a Safe Environment-The most important thing for your child to be healthy and happy is for the environment where they live and play to be safe. This means you want to keep breakable or**

dangerous items out of reach of children. During the toddler years children do not understand that something can hurt them and typically will play with anything they can reach. That includes the lighter that's just one drawer too low or the glass vase sitting on the coffee table. Those things can be moved back when your child gets old enough to understand the danger. For now, put them up higher where they can't be reached.

2. Use Non-Verbal 'Speech'- Though your child isn't old enough to express themselves in a clear way or to understand some of the words that you use they can be made to understand what you want from them through body language. This is because your child is born with great skills for reading your body language and when you are feeling a certain way you may be surprised at how well they pick up on it. Don't be afraid to use gestures or body language to convey your emotion or your intentions when teaching.

3. Teach Association Between Emotions and Feelings- When your child experiences something that makes them feel a certain way they may not necessarily understand what that feeling is. They know that they are feeling happy but they may not know the word for happy or they may not understand the best way to display that emotion. Try to anticipate the way your child is feeling and help them to understand it. For example on a holiday ask them 'are you happy you got a new toy?' They will be better able to understand what you're talking about when you associate it with something they are feeling at that moment. If you ask them 'do you like this new doll' while they are playing with it they can also associate the feeling better.

4. Teach Your Child to Walk the Right Way-Around

this age your child will be starting to walk for the first time. They will take their first steps with your help and by themselves and you want to make sure that you are teaching them properly. This means teaching them by holding their hands or letting them reach out and hold solid, unmovable objects such as tables or a couch. You don't want to use rolling toys because they provide an unnatural method of walking for your child and won't let them learn well. When they try to apply the skills from the toy to walking on their own they are more likely to stumble or fall and more likely to have difficulty.

5. Hold Conversations-You want your child to know how to communicate effectively with all different people. That means they need to know how to not only talk but listen as well. Teach them what two-sided conversations really are and how they work. This works best when you have a time that is quiet without distractions so that they can really focus on what you're saying (remember however that your child has a short attention span as a young child). As they get older this will become easier and will become more important as their near school age.

6. Read from the Start-Reading is something your child should know how to do as soon as possible. It's also something that you should do with your child as often as possible. You want them to learn to love reading and to learn new things constantly. By reading to your child from a young age that's exactly what they'll learn and it's exactly what they'll continue to do as they get older and start being able to read on their own. As soon as possible start teaching your child letters and sounds on the page and associate those words on the page with objects your child can see and feel. This helps them to form concrete images of what the words mean as

they read.

7. Provide Educational Toys-Educational toys vary from something that will teach your child colors or letters to ones that will teach animals or reading. These toys typically are brightly colored or sing or make other types of noise. They can teach your children better than anything else you could imagine because they let your child learn at their own pace and also allow them to feel independent as they work their way through.

8. Treat Separation Anxiety-The first time you leave your child somewhere by themselves you will probably feel separation anxiety. They will likely feel it too. Even if they have been at Grandma's house with you a million times they won't like being left there without you for the first time. Teach them to understand that even when you leave you are coming right back and you will not leave them forever. This can be done by leaving your child with your partner for a few minutes while you go do something outside or in another room. It can also help to leave your child for short periods of time in the beginning so they begin to associate your leaving with returning. Slowly they will begin to remember that you will come back and they will be more comfortable with the arrangement. It also helps to leave your child with someone they already know the first time you leave them.

9. Read, Read, Read-Did we mention reading? It's one of the most important things you can teach your child at this age because it's going to help them throughout the rest of their life. If they don't learn how to read at an early age it will be more and more difficult as time goes on. Reading is instrumental in our world and this means it's not something you want your child left behind on. Keep

pushing them to read and sound out words wherever you go. As them to read signs by the road or in the store and ask them to spell words for objects that you see such as a cat or dog. These things help them put letters together and understand the sounds. They also help your child understand that every object has a word and every word has letters that look a certain way.

10. Buy Proper Shoes-When your child first starts walking they are going to need support. Now support comes in two forms. One, you need to be there helping them and encouraging them as they try to do this on their own and two, they need shoes. Now when you have an infant you probably had shoes with soft bottoms that really were only there to keep their feet warm. After all they didn't walk then. Well now you're going to need shoes that provide support and help your child to walk the right way. Having incorrect shoes could actually cause them to walk improperly or even to get hurt when they try walking.

11. Help Your Child Be Independent-This may sound a little silly but it's very true. You want your child to understand that they are independent and that they can do things for themselves. When you help them to do something on their own it is not the same thing as doing it for them. You want to show them how they can do something like putting on their shoes or putting on a sweater. Show them how and then let them do it or tell them what to do and then sit back and watch. You will be there to provide assistance or direction if needed but they get to do the activity for themselves. This helps them feel self-satisfied and lets them believe they can do anything.

CHAPTER 4 - LOSING THE DIAPERS FOR GOOD – POTTY TRAINING 101

Now if you're like … well anybody, you're looking forward to the day when you no longer have to change a dirty diaper. Well when your child gets to this stage of their development that day is fast approaching. Many people like to try and rush this point of life by pushing their children to use the bathroom before they are ready. This is not going to help them progress faster in most cases and can actually hinder their ability to reach this stage.

So how do you know when your child is ready? They will tell you. Yes that's right your child will actually give you a very clear and informed acknowledgment that they are ready to use the bathroom. They will start to tell you when their diaper is dirty and needs to be changed and may even tell you that they want to use the 'big boy/girl potty.' When this happens you want to start teaching them right away. Girls will generally be ready around 18 months while boys are ready at around 22 (this is a very general range however so do not be overly concerned if your 20 month old girl is not showing signs yet or your 19 month old boy is).

1. **Give Your Undivided Attention-This is not the time to plan a get together with your friends or neighbors. When your child is ready to begin potty training you need to be able to pay attention to them and only them for the entire time. That means both when they are trying to use the potty and when they are going about the rest of their day. If your child says they need to go this also means that you need to immediately drop whatever you are doing and take them to the bathroom. Don't tell them to wait or try to make them 'hold it.' They aren't old enough to understand how to do this.**

2. **Start First Thing-First thing in the morning is generally when most people have to go to the bathroom for the first time. This means that as soon as you wake them up or as soon as they eat breakfast is the perfect time to take your child to the bathroom for the first time that day. Get them to sit on the potty for a few minutes even if they don't have to go (or say they don't have to go). You want to make sure you're giving them enough time to sit there and go if they have to but not so long it feels like a punishment.**

3. **Make Your Child Comfortable-Going to the bathroom on the potty when they've been wearing a diaper for a long time can be a strange experience. Your child likely wants to do it but they don't necessarily understand it and it may not be comfortable for them. Try to help your child relax by talking to them or reading them a story (maybe one about potty training for children). This makes it easier for them to actually go while they are on**

the potty instead of waiting until after.

4. Remind Your Child Frequently-When you're getting started with potty training it's very possible that your child will forget or will think of having to go too late to get to the potty. It might be a good idea to set yourself a reminder to take them into the bathroom for a few minutes every hour just to make sure they don't have to go. This can help prevent a lot of accidents and help your child master the skill faster than they would on their own.

5. Be Consistent-If you start potty training your child over the weekend and they still haven't learned by the next week you need to keep trying. Don't change the routine or decide that 'it's not going to happen.' You need to stay consistent and keep doing all the same things. This is a skill your child is learning and it may take them some time to completely master it. If you stop trying then they stop trying and that can actually cause them to feel upset or depressed because they feel like they have failed. Remember how we talked earlier about learning independence of not? Well this is one of those places where it happens.

6. Get Help-If you can't be there with your child 24/7 to make sure that you're always taking them to the potty every hour and any other time they need it then you need to make sure you have someone else that can. If someone doesn't take them when they need to go or they start having a lot of accidents because no one reminds them it can lead to the same depression or inadequacy feelings that we mentioned in point five. Getting someone else to help you doesn't make you a bad parent. It just means you realistically know you can't do it on your own. If you send your child to daycare you'll want to make sure they are

involved in the process as well.

7. Praise-Just like with anything else you teach your child make sure you use praise often. Every single time your child goes to the bathroom on the potty or tells you and makes it on time give them praise. That doesn't mean you have to give them a reward. It means telling them they did a good job. Even if they tell you but don't make it on time you want to praise them for knowing when they had to go. Each time you praise your child it reinforces the behavior and makes them want to do it again. This makes it easier for you to potty train your child. On the other side of things you want to make sure that you aren't punishing or scolding your child for not making it or not going when they are on the potty. Just tell them 'maybe next time' or 'that's okay.' You want them to understand that you still love them and that you are not mad so they will be more likely to try again.

CHAPTER 5- WHAT TO DO ABOUT BITING

So what do you do if your child turns out to be a biter? First of all why would your child bite another child or adult? Well much as your reaction to someone hurting you is to fight back, your child's reaction is also to retaliate. They do this in any way that they can which is where temper tantrums, pushing, hitting and biting all come into play. It's the same thing as when you yell, swear or hit the table in frustration. Your child is trying to express their strong emotions in the only way they know how.

The reasons for biting are many. Your child is different from other children and that means they may have different reasons for wanting to do something than another child. They may feel that they are out of control and therefore biting is retaliation. They may feel pain from teething in which case they often bite on anything that they can (toys, clothes, hands, and other people). They may even be craving attention or trying to interact. These things will all cause a child to bite or attack another person. But what can you do about it?

CHAPTER 6- FIXING THE BITING PROBLEM

The first thing you need to do is make sure that your child completely understands that biting is not okay and that you will not condone that behavior. If you aren't very firm on that point from the start then the behavior will not change. So how do you make sure that your child knows what they can and can't do? Well the first thing you need to do is verbally tell your child that biting is not acceptable.

You next want to make sure that you are providing your child with the right objects that they can bite. If they are unsure how to interact with people then it's likely that biting may be what they do simply for this reason. It's difficult to teach them how to interact if they are not given enough opportunities to talk with other people their own age. This means that it is important for your child to spend time with other children either in preschools, daycare or even in your neighborhood or with family.

By showing your child the best way to associate with others they will be able to associate meeting someone new with shaking hands or waving rather than biting. They will also be able to understand that certain things are for biting or are okay to bite while other things are not. However these are not the only things that you can do to help your child. The most important thing that you need to do is make sure that you're providing enough proper attention to your child so that they will feel like they get the attention they want.

Think about it this way, when your child does something wrong how much attention do you give them? How much attention do you give to them when you do something right? Are you giving more attention for the good things or the bad ones? Well if you're giving more attention to your child when they behave improperly you'll have a problem teaching them how to behave properly. That's because your child will do what they can to get the most attention whether it's positive or negative.

This means spending time with your child doing something positive. It means not just paying attention to them when they do something bad (or something good) but simply paying attention to them when they are just being them. Just sitting down and playing with your child will make your relationship with them better and it will make their relationships with others better as well.

So how can you spend time with your child in a positive way? The first thing to understand is what not to do. Spending time with your child in front of the TV (unless you're interacting with the child and the TV) is not the best way to spend time. Setting your child in front of the TV by themselves is not spending time with them either. And this is not good for their development either. You want to make sure that you are really talking with them while you play.

Some of the best ways to interact with your child are to do art projects such as finger-painting or play-dough. These things allow your child to express themselves and develop their imagination. They are also incredibly fun for you and your child and help the two of you spend time together in a positive way. You can even use this to help teach your child social skills such as holding two-sided conversations, or even learning different objects. For example you could ask your child to sculpt a dog or paint your house. These things allow them to really expand their abilities.

Even better than all of these things that your child will learn and that you will be able to do is the fact that you are increasing your child's intelligence and their emotional abilities by spending this time with them. This means they will have a step up when it comes time to start school or make new friends.

Bowe Packer

The last thing you need to make sure that you are doing is talking to your child when they are unhappy. Unhappiness can cause your child to bite for retaliation remember. This means that you need to teach your child what to do when they are angry or upset so that they will better understand the right action.

It's important that when your child is angry you talk with them about why they are angry. You want to ask them what happened and why they feel the way they do. Make sure that you don't belittle the way that they feel and that you try to explain to them what they should do when this happens the next time or when they feel this way again.

If they don't know how they should act or what they should do then they will likely have a hard time doing the right thing the next time. This means that not only will they bite the first time but they could bite again and again even though you have told them not to.

CHAPTER 7- WHY YOUR CHILD STARTS THROWING FITS

So here's the big problem. Your child at the age of two tends to throw temper tantrums that are much more flamboyant and loud than the temper tantrums they threw when they were younger. This is because your child now has a mind of their own, an opinion that is not always in line with yours and the vocabulary to make their opinions heard. This means that they will likely speak up about just about anything and just about everything simply because they can. This is something that can help them throughout their life but it can also make things quite difficult for you when they decide to be vocal.

A typical temper tantrum starts with your child not getting their way. From there they start screaming, yelling, hitting, kicking and throwing things. They tend to fight you or anyone that happens to be around them. They may decide to fight you about something as little as feeding them carrots instead of potatoes or making them wear an outfit that they don't like. All of these things could trigger a temper tantrum. It's also entirely possible that something that doesn't trigger a temper tantrum one day might do just that another. You never know what is going to make your toddler upset or how upset it will make them.

So what do you do when your child has a temper tantrum? Well the first thing you're going to want to make sure you do is remain calm. Your child will react better if you are relaxed and calm because you are where they will look for a reaction. If they are throwing a tantrum because they are angry then the fact that they are getting no reaction might keep them from prolonging the tantrum. If they are scared this will show them that there is nothing to be afraid of. The worst thing you can do is to physically hurt your child or react in anger. Make sure that you are responding in a positive way as well.

What you need to understand is that your child wants to get what they want or need. They are attempting to express that when they throw those temper tantrums which means that to help them stop the tantrum it is important that you find out what it is that they believe they want or need. Once you have determined this (which is typically easier after the child has calmed down) they will feel much better.

So how do you find out what they want before you calm them down when finding out is what calms them down? Well it's actually not as complicated as you may think. What you really need to do is make sure that you are listening to them and inform them that you want to help. When your child realizes that you are paying attention and working toward doing what they want then they will be more likely to relax. Tell the child that you would like to help but you don't understand them when they are crying. This will help them to understand what is wrong with their method of explaining.

Once the child is calm you want to sit down in a face-to-face manner and ask them what the problem is or what they would like. This allows them the opportunity to express their feelings and their desires in a calm manner. Once you know what they want you can respond to it. You want to use reinforcing statements such as 'I know you want a cookie but we are going to have dinner soon,' or 'I know that Julie has your new toy but she will give it back.' These statements show that you are listening to your child and you hear what they have to say. They also provide an answer to the problem.

If you are willing and able to give your child what it is that they need or want then you can give it to them at this point and inform them that next time they only need to ask. Reinforce this idea every time your child throws a temper tantrum for something that makes it unnecessary. Make sure also that you are not punishing temper tantrums with scolding or spanking because these typically only make the tantrum that much worse. You want to make sure you are being positive and helpful instead.

CHAPTER 8- KEEPING YOUR HOME SAFE FOR CHILDREN

Something you probably already think you know is that your home needs to be a safe environment for your child. You probably figure that you already have this all sorted out. You went through and put locks on your chemical cabinets and maybe put baby gates in areas where you don't want your child to go. But have you really done everything that needs to be done to keep your child safe? Chances are that there are things you haven't even thought of.

Children and toddlers especially love to explore their environment. They want to spend time looking at everything, touching, playing and usually putting them in their mouth. This means that you need to keep anything that could even remotely be dangerous to your child if they engaged in any of these things. It means that the bowl of colored stones on your table is a potential choking hazard and the pretty globe could easily be broken. Make sure that your child is not able to reach anything that could cause them harm.

You also need to think about your cupboards and drawers. If your child can reach them then it is highly likely that they will get into them, pull things out and experiment with them as well. So if you think you've hidden something away where your child won't find it you'll want to think again. Is the place it's hidden within reach of your little one's exploring hands? If the answer is yes than that item is not near as hidden as it needs to be.

Be careful that you are not assuming that you will watch your child all the time and be able to stop them from getting into things. There will be a moment or two where your child is out of your sight or where you turn your back for just one instant. Never underestimate the amount of time it takes for your child to get hurt or get into something dangerous. It can happen in only a split second. That's why so many products have been created for protection:

1. Door knob covers-Require you to push down on the cover while turning the knob so that little children can't open the doors easily.

2. Drawer/cabinet locks-Keep drawers/cabinets closed unless a special latch is engaged that is difficult for a child to engage.

3. Door alarms-Send a signal through the house if a door is opened so that children who are out of sight are still able to be monitored for exiting the home.

Of course these are only a few of the many products that are available to lock or secure everything in your home from the prying eyes and hands of your child. Certain products should always be watched over as well such as chemicals or household cleaners. These should definitely be locked away so that your child can't get to them easily and your child should be monitored whenever they are near these items just in case they manage to get into the lock.

Another thing to monitor is anywhere with water. This means anything from a bucket outside your home to the kiddie pool or bathtub. If you are not holding your child's hand or within touching distance these things should be completely emptied. This means that you never leave your child anywhere that water is kept or where they could easily fall into that water. It takes seconds for your child to drown and that's something that you never want to even think about.

When your child takes a bath you need to be immediately beside them at all times. Don't leave their side for a moment whether it's to get a towel or to answer the phone. You never want to even take your eyes off of them. Make sure that you also keep the water at a safe temperature and never above 120 degrees Fahrenheit. A good method of testing water is to use the inside of your wrist (like you do with baby bottles of formula) or your elbow. These are two very sensitive places on your body and they will register the heat faster than the palm of your hand or even the back of your hand.

Remember that nice new video game system your partner got for Christmas? Well it's something that your child will likely want to play with as well. Except their method of playing could involve throwing the controllers or trying to eat the games. They may knock over the console or pull on wires and cords. This means you want to keep those consoles as well as your DVD player and any other electronics out of their reach and away from those little hands. If they get into anything it will likely go in their mouth, and they may even try to push them over causing injury to themselves and to your electronics.

Two other things to think about very seriously are fireplaces and windows. You may not think about it but your child can very easily fall out of a window and get hurt. Even windows only a few inches off the ground could cause serious and permanent injury. As a result it's essential for you to keep those windows closed or closely observe your children.

Fireplaces should be avoided at all times with a small child. Never leave your child in a room with a fire without being in reach. You should always have some type of gate in front of the fireplace as well that will keep your child from getting too close to the heat. Even being near a fire could cause them harm without actually touching it. This is because the smoke and fumes of your fire could get into their nose, mouth and eyes. This can cause breathing problems or simply scare your child which should be avoided.

CHAPTER 9- HOW TO DISCIPLINE THE RIGHT WAY

Now we've mentioned a few times throughout this book so far that discipline and punishment are not the same thing. It's that age old saying that all punishment is discipline but not all discipline is punishment. You can teach your child without giving them punishment. It's important also however, to say that not all punishment is physical. This means that you don't have to physically spank your child in order to give them a punishment. Many other things could as punishment as well.

Your toddler will want to test the limits and push your buttons every now and then. They may try something just to see what will happen and the next time they may push it just a little bit further. Do you remember being a teenager and staying out just a few minutes past curfew? And when you didn't get in trouble or you only got scolded a little you may have stayed out just a little longer the next time and the next just to see what would happen. Well your toddler is very much the same way. They want to push the limits of what they are able and allowed to do just because they can.

Discipline techniques vary and the ones that work best for you will depend on the situation, the child and you. The important thing is to make sure that you are consistent in your discipline practices. If you aren't then it's possible that your child will continue doing the action because only sometimes do they get in trouble for it. You want them to know that a bad action is always bad and will always be disciplined.

CHAPTER 10- ON THE SPOT DISCIPLINE

So what do you want to do when you're trying to discipline your child? How are you going to teach them without resorting to punishment every time? Remember we said that punishment is something you only want to dole out when absolutely necessary. So what *should* you be doing to teach your child right and wrong? Before we start with that there are a few things you need to know about your child and what they need to be happy in their life.

1. Structure-Believe it or not children like for there to be consistency and routine in their lives. They like when bedtime comes at the same time and mom is always the one to get them up in the morning and breakfast is at the same time every day. Keeping those routines helps your child to do what needs to be done at the right times of the day. It also keeps them from being surprised.

2. Freedom-Your child wants to have a say in things whether it's determining which dress to wear or which toy to play with. They want to be able to make the decisions because it makes them feel more important. It also gives them a sense of control and that self-satisfaction that we talked about earlier. That doesn't mean you need to let them make all the choices and it doesn't mean you can't help guide those choices. Just letting them pick between two options will provide enough self-satisfaction for them.

3. Transparency-Your child wants to know what is expected of them when they do certain things or go certain places. If you tell them the rules then they will be more likely to follow them. Of course they won't always follow them either because they forget or because they are deliberately pushing the limits. When this happens you may want to give your child a

warning (for a minor break of the rules) or you may want to give more strict discipline. What you do not want to do is give in to what they want because they will learn that breaking the rules is acceptable and will not follow them the next time.

4. Safety-Your child trusts you to keep them safe. This is why they look to you when they are placed in a new environment or when someone new comes close to them. They trust you to provide what they need to feel safe and secure. If you are always the one providing safety to them then they will continue to trust you completely. This means keeping them away from dangerous situations even when you are outside of your own home. When you take them to visit someone for example you want to be sure that wherever you set them down to let them play they are not going to get into something that could hurt them.

5. Positivity-You need to keep a positive environment for your child and positive parenting as well. This means focusing on the good things your child does as well as explaining more often than punishing. If your child does something wrong for example it may momentarily stop them if you give a spanking. But your child has not learned anything except that you don't like that behavior. They still don't know what to do the next time the situation comes up which means they will repeat the same inappropriate behavior. What you need to do is inform your child that their action was wrong and tell them why. You also need to make sure you tell them what they should do if the situation happens again.

6. Love-Now this may seem like an obvious one because of course you love your child. You may be one of those parents that even tells their child every day or even multiple times a day that you love them but do

you say it when they misbehave? Do you give hugs when you scold your child? These are things that you should think about doing. When your child misbehaves and they are punished or scolded they will associate that action with how you feel about them. At the toddler stage of life your child doesn't understand that you still love them even when you are unhappy with them. They believe that being bad means you don't love them. That means you need to tell your child that you love them or give them a hug even after they have done something wrong and been disciplined for it.

CHAPTER 11- IGNORING YOUR CHILD PROPERLY

Now you're probably thinking, now it's time to get to the real information. Now I'm going to learn the big secret to how to discipline my child when they are misbehaving. Well that's true. We are going to talk about discipline. But you might be surprised at the two main ways that we believe are best for doing just that.

We are not going to look at physical punishments at all because these have been proven to actually cause more negative behavior. What we are going to look at instead are the two most common and most effective methods of getting your child to do what you want them to do.

The first of these is ignoring them. That's right you read that right. We're telling you that you can actually ignore your child when they do something that they are not supposed to be doing. This has to be done very carefully however because you want to be sure that your child is safe when you ignore them.

If they participate in an activity that could cause them harm or that could be dangerous you need to react quickly and effectively. If they are doing something improper that will not hurt them then it is okay to ignore them.

This works very well with temper tantrums as well. Your child may throw a temper tantrum because they are not getting what they want and they want you to pay attention to them and give them that item. If you ignore them it may cause the tantrum to escalate temporarily but if you continue to ignore them they will start to realize that they are not getting where they want to be. They will also realize that you are not going to give them the thing they want when they are acting that way and will try a new technique.

Ignoring your child also means that you completely ignore them. You need to be aware of what they are doing or what is happening to them while keeping your eyes away from them. Even if you do not respond, simply looking at your child will make them think that you are paying attention. This is where mastering the art of peripheral vision comes into play. Make sure you can see your child and see that they are safe without them knowing you see them.

Another bad behavior that can be treated this way is inappropriate words. When you react strongly to your child using 'mean' words or 'bad' words you are actually enforcing their use. They will pick up these words from you or from others they hear and may not even understand what they really mean or how to use them but they will try.

Just like they try using all the other words they pick up from you in conversation they will use bad words as well. If you ignore the word then they start to see it as a 'wrong' word. Instead of being bad it's a word that doesn't work or doesn't mean anything. It doesn't get what they want and so it shouldn't be used.

Chapter 12- Teaching Timeouts

The second method of teaching your child is with timeouts. When you give a timeout for a negative behavior you are providing them with a time to sit and think about the action that they have just done or what they have just said and why it was bad. You want to enforce this by talking to your child before and after the timeout.

Let's say you just saw your two year old child push their cousin while playing. You want to immediately take them by the hand and get them to a quite area away from everyone else. Make sure they are looking at you and tell them that it is not okay to push people and you want them to sit in the corner, chair, etc. for two minutes (one minute for each year of age) and think about what they did and what they should do next time.

Once the two minutes is up (you can use a watch or kitchen timer to tell when time is up) walk over to them and talk to them about what they did and what they should do. If they pushed because the other child took their toy away tell them next time to simply ask for it back or to share the toy. Make sure they understand what it was they did wrong, why they were put in timeout and what they need to do to have a better outcome.

Once your conversation is over you want to give them a hug or kiss and let them know that you still love them and that they did good by sitting in timeout or by knowing what they did wrong and let them go back and play. The timeout is over and it's also forgotten. That means you don't mention it again and you don't punish them again for what they've already sat in timeout for (unless they do it again).

So you may be thinking, what if my child gets up from that timeout and won't sit still? Well first of all you want to make sure you tell your child as soon as you sit them down exactly how long they have to sit. Leaving this open-ended makes your child feel like they are sitting forever and they definitely won't sit still then. So tell them 'you need to sit here for two minutes and think about what you did.' If they get up before you tell them they can you need to take them by the hand and silently sit them back down and then start the clock over again.

This means your child will actually sit completely still in the spot you put them for the full amount of time. Every time they get up you put them right back. The important thing is not to engage them at all when you do this. You don't want them to feel like they are getting away with anything by doing this. It

Bowe Packer

may take an hour to get your child to sit still for two minutes, be willing to take that entire time if need be.

CHAPTER 13- LOOK FOR THE BEST IN THE WORST

The terrible twos are a terrible time for a lot of parents but they don't have to be the worst years of your life. They can be better than you may have thought if you simply put some effort into it and work hard at keeping your child happy and healthy as we've stressed throughout this book. The most important focuses are discussed in the next sections but for now we're going to talk about keeping a positive attitude.

Of course you're going to have problems when your children reach this age. You're going to wish that they would stop doing the things that annoy you and that they would listen when you tell them to do things. But what you're really going to need to do is make sure that you and your child are having the best time possible because they are only going to be at this stage once and though you'll remember these years as bad, you'll also remember them with fondness and wish you could go back.

So what should you do when your child is at their absolute worst and you're thinking you just can't handle it anymore? Look for that silver lining in the clouds and think about the best way to look at it. Think about what your child is learning or accomplishing by acting the way that they do and understand that it's not just about being a perfect child. Your child learns by misbehaving and by getting into things they shouldn't.

When they draw on the wall they are expressing their creativity and their imagination. Even though you find it wrong and you get upset they see it as art and they feel as though they are expressing themselves. The truth is that they really are expressing themselves and though you shouldn't encourage them to draw on the wall you should encourage them to keep drawing on paper.

Saying no is a big part of the terrible twos and one of the parts that most parents find to be the absolute worst. Your child may even start telling you no without really knowing what they are saying no to. The important thing is that your child is learning to express themselves and learning to have a mind of their own. This means that you don't have a child who is going to be a little sheep and do whatever the main group is doing. They are going to forge their own path.

Though it may seem annoying to you when your child refuses to eat their green beans or insists that they wear the red pants with the camo shirt, they are actually making great strides towards being their own person and creating their own identity. This is something that should actually be encouraged (though not every time your child says no are you going to want to let them have their way).

Another important aspect of your child's development is when they start getting into things. How often do you have to pull your child out of their closet to stop playing with the clothes or out of the flower pot to stop playing with dirt? These things are messy and taking care of these things can cause you some great difficulty but your child is learning things every time they do this. They don't necessarily realize that what they do causes trouble for you and they don't intend to upset you. They are simply trying to understand their world.

By exploring your child learns the best way to do all the things they want to do in life. They also learn more about the world in general. For example your child learns that plants need dirt to grow and that dirt has bugs in it. They learn that their clothes are different from each other and that each piece looks different as well. If your child is not in danger it's best to let them do as much exploring as possible so that they get the most out of their world.

The last thing to think about is learning from your child. When you look at your toddler what do you see? They are generally very happy, smiley and friendly. They want everyone to talk to them and they want everyone to like them. But they are also very open. You may find yourself embarrassed as your child tells a family secret to a complete stranger or you may find your child laughing one minute and crying the next.

All of these things happen because of the natural personality your child was born with. You can learn from this. Over time society tends to change people until they stop trusting instinctively and start hiding their true emotions under layers of uncertainty. Look at your child and try to be like them instead of letting them always take after you.

Instead of shying away from that friendly man on the subway give him a chance and share a smile and maybe a story or two. Instead of hiding when your friend says something you don't like let them know how you feel. You'll feel much better and you'll actually have a better time in life as well.

Chapter 14- Keeping Your Child (and You) Stress-Free

The final thing we have to talk about are the main aspects to focus on in your child's life and the life that you are building together. You want to remember each of these things as you continue to raise them and they continue to grow. By learning these key aspects of development and growth you can best teach your child and help them turn into great, well-rounded adults.

Focus #1: Be Consistent
Like we mentioned before your child likes things to happen in a routine fashion. They don't like when you change the plan out of the blue. If you always get breakfast right after waking up but you decide to go to the store first you might find yourself with a very angry two-year-old. The same happens with many other situations. Your child does not like changes to happen in their life because these things make it difficult to predict what will happen next. Also, if one thing can change then it means that everything in their life can change and they don't know what to expect for anything in life.

Focus #2: Keep Stressful Situations at a Minimum
Having a stress-free life with your child means keeping out a lot of the stressful things that happen in life. This means avoiding a lot of those sudden changes or interruptions to the routine. It also means making sure that your child's basic needs are met. Make sure they are not tired or hungry or bored. You want to keep them to a regular nap schedule and feeding schedule as well. When you skip these times your child is more likely to be upset or have a tantrum.

Now this is not to say that you can't ever change the routine or you can't ever do something new. Change is something your child will need to learn to understand but you want to make sure that too many changes are not occurring at once. When too many changes happen altogether your child will feel blindsided and upset. When only one or two things are changed (minor changes) they will likely be upset but more consolable.

Focus #3: Walk a Mile in Their Shoes
When you start to get frustrated with your child's actions think about what they are feeling. Try to understand why they are acting the way they do and what they might be thinking at the time. Maybe your child has a valid reason for why they are acting the way that they are or at least it seems that way to them. If this is the case then you will want to make sure you are addressing the problem before reacting in a negative way. You definitely don't want to teach your child that they should not react when something is wrong.

Focus #4: Use the Short Attention Span
A two-year-old child does not have a very good attention span. This is why you keep time-outs to such a short length. After two minutes your two-year-old has forgotten what they did wrong. So how can you use that attention span when normally it's so distracting and problematic for you? Well it works great when your child is doing something you don't want them to do.

Think about it this way; your child is throwing their cereal all over the living room but when you try to take the bowl they scream and cry. You don't want them making a mess but you also don't want to invite a temper tantrum. So what do you do? If you offer your child something else, say a car or a book, they will likely forget about that bowl of cereal so that you can take it away and get rid of it. They have been sufficiently distracted.

Focus #5: Find a Safe Place
Once again keeping your child safe is key. You never want to leave them alone in a situation where they are capable of getting into danger. When your child gets hurt and you allow it to happen they start to mistrust you. Once that mistrust begins it is difficult to change. You want them to feel like they are safe with you and like you will always do whatever you can to protect them and keep them safe.

There is more to this type of safety however than just being safe in their home. Your child should have a space that is completely safe to them. This might mean a special corner of the house that they go to when they are upset or want to be 'alone.' It might be a hidden corner or even hiding under a blanket in their room. All of these things could be an area that your child feels is protected enough that they can go there whenever they are upset and not have to worry.

Focus #6: Remain Calm
When your child is hurt or when they are acting in a way that you don't approve of it can be very difficult to keep your cool. You want to scream and yell and you may feel that punishment is the best option to curb the behavior but this is not the case. What you want to do instead is stay calm and try to instill that calmness on your child as well.

By staying calm you are telling your child that what they are doing is not working to get attention or get a 'rise' out of you. You are effectively telling them that they are not going to succeed at what they are doing by simply screaming or throwing tantrums.

Focus #7: Give in to Demands
Now we've all seen those parents whose child throws a huge tantrum in the store and they decide to give the child what they wanted. This isn't good parenting and it's not something that we recommend you do. On the other hand if your child is asking for something that isn't going to cause harm then it isn't a bad idea to give in once in a while.

Now the key here is 'once in a while.' You don't want your child to think that they can get their way all the time. You want to instill in them that you are still in charge and that you make the rules so they know that they can't always get what they want. By teaching them that asking nicely gets them a better chance of getting what they want however, you have a lesser chance of experiencing temper tantrums.

CHAPTER 15- KEEP THE LINES OPEN

In closing it's important to talk about communication skills. Your child is important and they want to feel that way. You may feel like you are giving your child the attention that they need but it may not come across that way to them. This means you need to show them that they are important and that you are listening when they talk to you. So how do you go about doing that?

There are a few different things you need to do when your child attempts to speak with you. One is that you need to put down what you are doing and give them your undivided attention. That means you don't look at your phone or work on dinner or anything else for the span of time that it takes to talk to them. If you don't have a moment to spare at that exact time then tell them to wait five minutes (or ten, etc.) and come back so you can give them your full attention.

If your child knows that you aren't blowing them off (you gave them a definite time to come back and a reason why they need to come back) they are more likely to feel appreciated and important even though you told them not to talk to you at that moment. This is because you want to give your child true feedback for what they are saying and not just nod and grunt along.

Chances are pretty good that your child is trying to tell you something that won't require a lot of your time. At this stage of their life your child is looking for feedback on just about everything that they do which means they could come running to tell you that it's five steps from the couch to the chair or that they can jump really high. These things are important to your child even if they are not important to you and it's important that you show interest in what your child has to say to you.

No matter what they are saying or what you think they are going to say it's important that you wait for your child to be done talking before you speak. Even though you need to display positive and active listening your child will not understand if you interrupt them to ask questions and may forget what they were saying. Unlike talking with adults, this type of interaction is not encouraged with children. You want them to feel like you are completely focused on them however so make sure you let them say everything they want to say and that your body language shows you are engaged in the conversation.

Keep serious conversations for just you and your child. These conversations could be embarrassing for your child even if the topic is not actually embarrassing. This is because your child starts to feel and understand shame at this stage in their life and feels it very strongly when they are young. Any conversation in front of company or strangers could embarrass them.

Using negative labels makes your child feel as though those labels are correct. Your child will likely not have much of a self-concept of themselves. They don't know what they think of themselves and they don't know who they really are yet. That means your opinion is the one they base those things off of. If you tell them they are stupid they start to believe it because you know better than they do (or so they assume).

Finally, make sure you are listening actively. This means you're not just somewhat paying attention but you're truly listening and understanding. You want to repeat back what they say to you and give them feedback on it so they know you really did hear and you really do care. This makes your child more likely to talk to you about things the next time and gives them the skills they need to talk to others as well.

ABOUT THE AUTHOR

Hello, my name is Bowe Chaim Packer and I like to see myself as an open, "***wear my heart out on my sleeve***" kind of guy.

Some of the most important things to me in my life are:

- Laughing
- Kissing
- Holding hands
- Being playful
- Smiling
- Talking deeply with others
- Being loved
- Loving others
- Changing the world one person at a time (if my presence in your life doesn't make a difference then why am I here?) Hmmmmm, maybe that is a topic for another book. ;-)
- Learning from others (although often times I first resist). However, don't give up on me….
- Sharing ideas (no matter what they might be)
- Learning about others via most forms of contact.
- Traveling – hello, of course – almost forgot one of my favorite pass times.

Remember, LIFE is a journey for each and every one of us. We must never forget the things that are important to us or lose sight of what makes us happy.

Made in the USA
Middletown, DE
07 September 2022

73330138R00035